W9-CKH-962

Online
Safety

by Sarah L. Schuette

PEBBLE
a capstone imprint

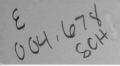
Little Pebble is published by Pebble
1710 Roe Crest Drive
North Mankato, Minnesota 56003
www.mycapstone.com

Library of Congress Cataloging-in-Publication Data
Names: Schuette, Sarah L., 1976– author.
Title: Online safety / by Sarah L. Schuette.
Description: North Mankato, Minnesota : An imprint of Pebble, [2020] |Series: Little Pebble. Staying safe! | Audience: Age 6–8. | Audience: K to Grade 3. | Includes bibliographical references and index. Identifiers: LCCN 2018052363| ISBN 9781977108685 (hardcover) | ISBN 9781977110299 (paperback) | ISBN 9781977108760 (ebook pdf) Subjects: LCSH: Internet—Safety measures—Juvenile literature. Classification: LCC TK5105.875.I57 S393 2020 | DDC 005.8—dc23
LC record available at https://lccn.loc.gov/2018052363

Editorial Credits
Erika L. Shores, editor; Heidi Thompson, designer; Morgan Walters, media researcher; Marcy Morin, scheduler; Tori Abraham, production specialist

Photo Credits
All photos by Capstone Studio/Karon Dubke

All internet sites appearing in back matter were available and accurate when this book was sent to press.

The author dedicates this book to her nieces, Ali and Tes Eilers.

Capstone thanks Shonette Doggett, coalition coordinator, Safe Kids Greater East Metro/St. Croix Valley, St. Paul, Minnesota, for reviewing this book.

Printed and bound in China.
001671

Table of Contents

Be Smart 4

Follow Rules 12

Be Safe 20

Glossary 22
Read More 23
Internet Sites 23
Critical Thinking Questions . . 24
Index 24

Be Smart

Be smart.

Follow rules

for being online.

Internet Safety Tips

* Do not chat with strangers online.

Keep your personal information private. *

* Be nice to people.

If you ever feel uncomfortable, tell a grown up. *

5

Cal uses a tablet.

He asks before

he goes online.

Lola talks to her dad.
He tells her what
websites are safe.

Connor wants to play

a new game. Wait!

He must ask first.

Follow Rules

Think!

Sam thinks before he types.

He's careful with his words.

He is kind.

Ali never gives out
her name.

Her address is private too.

Nala never posts
her picture.

She keeps herself safe.

Tes keeps her passwords safe. She only tells her mom or dad.

Be Safe

Are you safe online?

PLAYER INFO

ADD YOUR INFO TO UNLOCK PRIZES

NAME

ADDRESS

NO THANKS

Glossary

online—to be connected to the internet

password—a secret code made up of letters, words, or numbers

private—not meant to be shared

tablet—a computer device that is flat and shaped like a magazine or pad of paper; a tablet is used to go on the internet, watch videos, or play games

website—a place on the internet with facts, games, or pictures

Read More

Atkins, Marcie Flinchum. *Be Smart Online*. Rookie Get Ready to Code. New York: Children's Press, 2019.

Gifford, Clive. *Super Social Media and Awesome Online Safety*. Get Connected to Digital Literacy. New York: Crabtree, 2018.

Miller, Shannon. *Staying Safe Online*. Library Skills. North Mankato, MN: Cantata Learning, 2018.

Internet Sites

McGruff Safe Kids
https://www.mcgruff-safe-kids.com/2014/08/10-internet-safety-tips-for-kids/

NetsSmartz: Know the Rules
https://www.netsmartz.org/etSmartzKids/KnowTheRules

Super-cool stuff!

Check out projects, games, and lots more at
www.capstonekids.com

Critical Thinking Questions

1. What should you do before you type?

2. What should you do if you want to play a new game online?

Index

addresses, 14

asking, 6, 10

names, 14

passwords, 18

pictures, 16

posting, 16

rules, 4

tablets, 6

typing, 12

websites, 8